A Sense of Science
Exploring Materials

Claire Llewellyn

W
FRANKLIN WATTS
LONDON•SYDNEY

This edition 2011 published by
Franklin Watts
338 Euston Road
London NW1 3BH

Franklin Watts Australia
Level 17/207 Kent Street
Sydney NSW 2000

Editor: Jeremy Smith
Art Director: Jonathan Hair
Design: Matthew Lilly
Cover and design concept:
Jonathan Hair
Photography: Ray Moller
unless otherwise stated.

Photograph credits:
Alamy: 7t, 9t, 23b, 27b.

We would like to thank Scallywags
for their help with the models in
this book.

A CIP catalogue record
for this book is available
from the British Library.

Dewey classification: 620.1'1

ISBN: 978 1 4451 0632 8

Printed in China

Franklin Watts is a division
of Hachette Children's Books,
an Hachette UK company.
www.hachette.co.uk

Contents

Material world

Every day we use all sorts of things. They are made of different materials.

Glass mirror

Plastic toothbrush

Metal tap

Cotton towel

We use lots of
materials in
our home.

Feel it
Ask a friend to
collect four
things made of
different
materials. With
your eyes shut,
can you say what
the materials
are?

How many different
materials can
you see at
school?

Rough or smooth

Materials can feel rough or smooth.

A glass window feels very smooth.

Rough or smooth?

Feel a paper towel with your finger tips. Then feel the paper on this page. Which one is rougher? Which one is smoother?

A tree
feels rough.

It is nice
to sit on
a smooth
wooden
seat.

Warm or cold

Materials can
feel warm
or cold.

Glass feels colder than plastic.

A teddy
feels warm.

On your feet
Stand on a hard floor in your bare feet.
Now stand on some carpet. Which feels
warmer?

Stretchy and bendy

Some materials can bend or stretch.

A plastic phone lead bends this way and that.

S-t-r-e-t-c-h

Find an elastic band and guess how far it will stretch. Now try it: were you right?

This rubber cap is soft and stretchy.

This plastic
helmet is not.

Waterproof materials

Some materials are waterproof. They do not let water through.

Wet or dry?
Fill a rubber glove with water. What happens?

A plastic shelter keeps out the rain.

You can carry a drink around in a plastic bottle.

Magnetic materials

Many things are made of metal. Some of them will stick to a magnet.

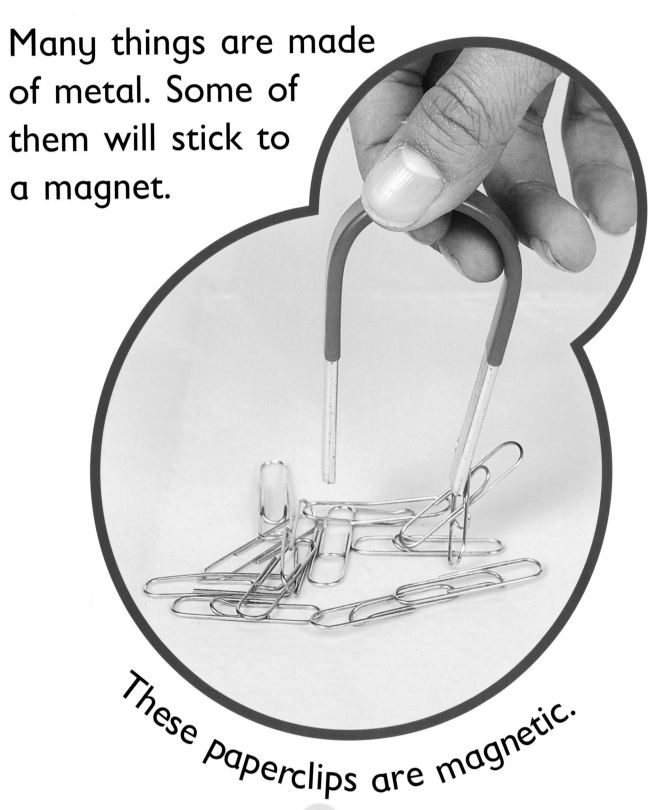

These paperclips are magnetic.

Other materials
are not
magnetic.

Stick up!
Find a fun
magnet and try
to stick it
around the
house. Where
will it stick?
Where won't
it?

These magnetic
animals are sticking
to the fridge door.

Strong or not?

Some materials are very strong.

We can lie on a strong wooden bed.

This plastic bag is very strong.

Paper play

Get some card and some newspaper. Fold each one and try to stand it up. What happens?

This paper bag is not.

Can you see through it?

Some materials
are transparent.
We can see through them.

In the bag

Get a transparent plastic bag and a bag made of paper. Put some things inside each one. What do you notice?

We can't see what is inside the box.

We can see what is inside the jar.

Natural materials

Some materials are made by nature.

Wood comes from trees.

Exploring wood

Find a piece of wood from outside. What does it look and feel like? Does it look and feel like wood in your home?

Sheep and other animals give us wool.

People make pots from clay, which is dug from the ground.

Made by people

Some materials are made by people.

Plastic hunt

Find three different things made of plastic. Do they look and feel the same?

Plastic is made in a factory.

It is made from oil that looks like this.

Plastic can be made into lots of different items.

Choosing the right materials

We need to choose materials carefully.

Plastic is good for outdoor toys because it does not spoil in the rain.

Wool is good for clothes because it is warm.

Shape it
Play with some Plasticine (or other modelling material) What is it like? What can it do? What can you make with it?

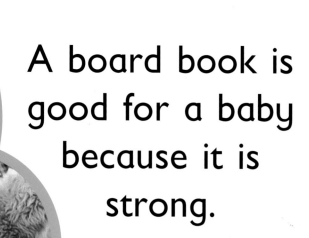

A board book is good for a baby because it is strong.

Glossary

Factory A place where things are made by machines.

Magnetic Something that will stick to a magnet.

Natural Made by nature.

Stretch To make something longer or wider by pulling on it.

Transparent Something that you can see through, like glass.

Waterproof Something that will not let water through, like a plastic umbrella.

Wooden Made of wood.

Wool The fur of a sheep.

Material hunt

1. Choose a material, such as wood, plastic or metal.

2. Go on a hunt around the house and try and find ten small items made of your material.

3. Arrange your items on a table top or tray.

4. Look at the items hard for a minute and then cover them with a cloth. Can you remember what was there?

Index